ROME

A Picture Book to Remember Her by

CRESCENT BOOKS
NEW YORK

CLB 1606
© 1987 Illustrations and text: Colour Library Books Ltd.,
   Guildford, Surrey, England.
Text filmsetting by Acesetters Ltd., Richmond, Surrey, England.
All rights reserved.
Printed and bound in Barcelona. Spain by Cronion, S.A.
1987 edition published by Crescent Books, distributed by Crown Publishers, Inc.
ISBN 0 517 61401 4
h g f e d c b a

It is almost certain that more words have been written about Rome than about any other city on earth, and this is hardly surprising. Even today it still casts its spell, still remains 'The Eternal City', the city to which all roads lead. And when we look back across the centuries it is not difficult to see why: there was a time when all roads did, indeed, lead, however circuitously, to the hub of a mighty empire whose jurisdiction reached to the very corners of the known world. Rome's laws, architecture, art, statesmanship and civilization were spread by its ambition, through the medium of the most formidable armies the world had seen, led by equally formidable generals, throughout the empire. Rome's influence was enormous, and the legacy of that influence remains with us to this day.

Coincidental with the eventual decline of its territorial empire, Rome took on the role of capital of the Holy Roman Empire, assuming its position as the seat of Christianity, and this, an equally potent force for change, it also spread throughout the world.

It is when we consider the size of Ancient Rome that our wonder increases. How could such a relatively small city, with its relatively small population, achieve such eminence and power? We can only marvel at the tenacity of purpose, the determination, the singlemindedness, that made all this possible, for a city with such humble beginnings as a settlement on the River Tiber in the 8th century BC.

Legend tells us that Rome was founded by Romulus, the first of a succession of seven kings. History records that its empire dates from 30 BC when, following the assassination of Julius Caesar, his adoptive son Octavian, later to rule Rome for forty one years as the Emperor Augustus, defeated his rival Mark Anthony at Actium. It was in the early part of the 2nd century AD that Rome achieved the greatest extent of empire, under the Emperor Trajan.

Today, Rome is no longer the hub of empire in the way that we understand empire, but its compelling attraction, through the Vatican City on the one hand, and the awe with which we still regard the achievements of Ancient Rome on the other, remains just as strong as ever.

It would be hard to imagine that anyone would visit Rome and not wish to see its antiquities, but that is not to say there is nothing more to Rome. Far from it. Rome is beautiful, superbly situated, at times quaint, at times grand and imposing, and always displaying an elegance all its own. It may be that all roads no longer lead to Rome, but for the traveller they certainly should.

The Basilica of St. Peter's.

The Basilica of St. Peter's, with its ornate facade (top and previous pages) and inside, seen through the Nave (above), the Bronze Canopy, above which is the magnificent Dome (right), designed by Michelangelo.

Above: the Basilica of St. John in Lateran. Right: a Swiss Guard in his colourful dress. Centre right: the Bernini Colonnade. Inside St. Peter's (far right) are many exquisite works of art, including a copy (top right) of Domenichino's depiction of St. Jerome's last communion. Overleaf: (bottom left) people gaze in wonder at the frescoes of the Sistine Chapel, one of the Vatican's greatest treasures. Also in the Vatican is the Pinacoteca, which houses Bellini's *Pietà* (top left) and Raphael's *The Transfiguration of Christ* (top right). Bottom right: *The Miracles of St. Frances Ferreri* by Francesco del Cossa.

The museums in the Vatican City (these pages)
contain the world's largest collection of
antiquities, with each room overflowing with
artistic treasures of exceptional beauty. Top: the
Chiaramonti Museum, which houses the *Nile* (right).
Above: the Gallery of Maps. St. Peter's Square
(overleaf), is bounded by Bernini's marvellous
elliptical Colonnade and contains two fountains,
one by Maderno, the other by Bernini, on either
side of the 85-foot-tall obelisk, which was brought
from Egypt by Caligula in 38 A.D.

Horse-drawn cabs (top and right) provide a pleasant mode of transport for tourists. Although very different, the facades of St. Peter's (right) and of the 16th century church of Trinità dei Monti (above), were both designed by one artist, Maderno. Overleaf: the Tiber, spanned by Ponte Sant'Angelo, with Castel Sant'Angelo on the right and the white dome of St. Peter's beyond the bridge.

Above: a couple succumbs to the romance of Rome. Top left: Castel Sant'Angelo. Centre right: Ponte Fabricio and (left) Ponte Cestio, both of which lead to Isola Tiberina (remaining pictures), the Tiber's only island.

The splendour of Rome is not only contained in its museums and galleries, for priceless works of art are to be found all over the city in the statuary (these pages) adorning bridges, squares and fountains.

Although in ruins, the Forum
(these pages) still conveys the
glory of Imperial Rome. Below:
the Temple of Vesta. Right: the
Arch of Constantine and
(remaining pictures) the marble
Arch of Septimius Severus.

The 4th century Basilica of Maxentius (below), Caesar's Forum (centre right) and the Arch of Titus (bottom right) are some of the fascinating ruins contained in the Forum (previous pages). Overlooking them is probably the most famous symbol of Rome's former glory, the mighty Colosseum, or Flavian Amphitheatre (left and overleaf).

The disciplined design of the Colosseum (these pages) originally consisted of three storeys when it was built by Vespasian in AD 72. Eight years later, when another storey had been added by his son Titus, the massive, elliptical amphitheatre was inaugurated. It was 159 feet high, 558 feet long and capable of holding a crowd of 50,000. Today, despite its decay, the remarkable elegance of the building still inspires awe.

Roman ruins, such as the
Forum (previous pages and
above) and the Colosseum
(right) attain their full,
magical splendour when seen
floodlit at night. The
church of San Paolo fuori le
Mura (facing page) was
originally built by
Constantine the Great in 324
over the tomb of the Apostle
Paul. The present building
dates from the 1850s and is
one of Rome's most beautiful
churches, with its elegant
facade topped by a mosaic of
gold and rich colours.
Overleaf: as lightning
flashes, speeding vehicles
produce red streaks of light
on the Via del Foro, which
is flanked by the ruined
Temples of Saturn and
Vespasian.

Above: a view of Piazza del Popolo, with its 24-metre-high Egyptian obelisk, which was erected by Pope Sixtus V in 1589. Left: Michelangelo's *Tiber*. Below: the Temple of Vesta, its design influenced by Greek art, is so called due to its similarity to the original Temple of Vesta which stands in ruins in the Forum. Bottom left: the lovely gardens of the Villa Borghese, where the Galleria Borghese houses several fine masterpieces by artists such as Raphael, Bernini, Caravaggio and Titian. Facing page: the Palatinum, in the Forum.

Far left: an old Roman street and (top centre) a mosaic at the Baths of Neptune in Ostia. Remaining pictures: the 2nd century AD Hadrian's Villa , with its lovely Canopus Canal (left).

The main attraction of the
town of Tivoli, some 30km
from Rome, is the Villa
d'Este (facing page, inset)
with its famous garden
(these pages). Exemplifying
the 'Italianate Style',
these beautifully landscaped
grounds contains some
spectacular fountains such
as those on the Hundred
Fountains Alley (below) and
the Organs Fountain (facing
page). The Capitol, with its
splendid Senator's Palace
(overleaf), was once the
spiritual centre of Rome.
The huge statues of the twin
gods Castor and Pollux flank
Michelangelo's magnificent
stairway, the Cordonata,
which leads to the Capitol.

Above: the Temple of Vespasian. Facing page, top left: Bernini's Colonnade. The impressive Monument to Victor Emmanuel II (remaining pictures), built to celebrate the 50th anniversary of the Kingdom of Italy, is decorated by many splendid statues, including *Patriotism Triumphant* (facing page, top right).

Previous pages: the Monument to Victor Emmanuel II, which is also known as 'Vittoriano'. One of Rome's best-loved fountains is the *Fountain of the Moor* (these pages), which was designed by Bernini, and erected by Mari. It is seen (right) in Navona Square with the famous *Fountain of the Four Rivers* beyond.

One of the three fountains in Navona Square (these pages) is the *Fountain of Neptune* (bottom and facing page), erected in the 19th century.

Apart from Rome's fascinating history and wealth of artistic treasures, the vitality and colour of the city is an integral part of its charm. On market days, the muted hues of the ancient streets and squares provide a backdrop for brightly coloured stalls overflowing with glorious flowers and fresh produce.

Left: an art exhibition decorates the Spanish Steps, a famous Baroque staircase rising from the fashionable Piazza di Spagna. Characteristic of Rome is the sight of its citizens socialising and relaxing on the streets, outside cafés or bars (below), while horse-drawn cabs (remaining pictures) are also one of the city's everyday sights.

POETI DI ARTISTI DI EROI
NSATORI DI SCIENZIATI
RI DI TRASMIGRATORI

Within Rome's suburbs (top left) one can find modern architecture of great beauty, such as the Palazzo della Civiltà (top) and the Church of Ss. Peter and John (above), both in the E.U.R. suburb (bottom far left). Left: a typical, lively Roman cafe. Overleaf: sunset over the Tiber and (following page) the Spanish Steps.